COLOSSAL CONSTRUCTIONS

THE POWER OF
PYRAMIDS

by Thea Feldman

SUPERSCRAPERS

by Chana Stiefel

CONTENTS

THE POWER OF
PYRAMIDS

SUPERSCRAPERS

THE POWER OF PYRAMIDS

by Thea Feldman

CHAPTER 1

WHAT IS A PYRAMID?

Have you ever noticed that different kinds of buildings have different shapes? Many sports stadiums are oval. An oval shape allows more people to have a good view of what's happening on the field. **Architects** often design rectangular schools and houses. Rectangular or square rooms fit well together and make good use of space.

Do you know how a pyramid is shaped? Pyramids have triangular sides that meet at a point at the top. Some of the earliest large structures were pyramids. The pyramids of ancient Egypt may be the best-known early pyramids. They have been pictured in countless movies, magazines, and books. We are fascinated by their unusual shape, tremendous size, and great age.

Building a large structure in the shape of a pyramid was an enormous **architectural** challenge for the Egyptians. So why did they create pyramids? As you read this book, you will learn why the ancient Egyptians were gripped by the power of the pyramid.

The Egyptian pyramids were all designed with four identical triangular sides and a square foundation or base. The four sides meet at a point at the top of the pyramids. Egyptian pyramids were the tallest human-made buildings of their time. They were built thousands of years ago, yet many are still standing today. What was the purpose of these pyramids?

An Egyptian pyramid was a monument built for a pharaoh. A pharaoh was the king of ancient Egypt. After a pharaoh died, his body was treated in a special way. He became a mummy, a dead body that has been carefully preserved. A pharaoh's mummy was buried in a **tomb** located deep beneath a pyramid. Only pharaohs had such special burial places. About 90 pyramids were built to honor Egypt's pharaohs. Most of these were built more than 4,500 years ago.

Ancient pyramids are not **confined** to Egypt, though. Did you know that pyramids have been found in other places around the world? The largest pyramid outside of Egypt is in Mexico, halfway around the world.

There were many pyramids built in the area known today as Latin America. They were located in Mexico, Guatemala, Belize, El Salvador, Honduras, and Peru. Some were built more than 1,500 years ago. Latin American pyramids are not very old compared to Egyptian pyramids.

Other people in other places built pyramids, too. For instance, the ancient Kushite people built even more pyramids than the Egyptian people. The Kushites lived south of Egypt in a region known as Nubia. Kushite pyramids were built much later than the Egyptian ones.

In Mesopotamia, people built ziggurats. Ziggurats were tall buildings with triangular sides. Just like the Egyptian and Latin American pyramids, some ziggurats still stand to this day. It is amazing that these ancient buildings have managed to avoid complete **destruction** after so many centuries.

In each culture, the pyramid had its own unique shape. Yet pyramids around the world clearly **resemble** one another. Do you find this surprising? Most of these cultures did not know about one another, but they all built pyramid-shaped monuments. That says a lot about pyramid power!

The most famous Egyptian pyramids still stand at Giza today.

Chapter 2
AN AFTERLIFE FIT FOR A KING

Most of the pointed pyramids of ancient Egypt were built for pharaohs who ruled from 2575 to 2134 BCE. The early Egyptians trusted their pharaohs completely. They believed the pharaohs were more than simply kings. They believed their pharaohs were gods in human form.

Gods and religion were very important to early Egyptians. They thought their gods were **involved** in almost every part of daily life. Ra was one of the most important gods. Egyptian pictures of Ra show him with a man's body and a falcon's head. Ra was the sun god. The sun was a very important symbol of rebirth. When the sun set each night, it "died." The following morning the sun lived again.

Ancient Egyptians believed that pharaohs were Ra's sons. Egyptians thought pharaohs deserved a special burial place because they were gods. The pharaoh's pyramid was also seen as a special place he would need after he died. The ancient Egyptians believed in life after death or an afterlife. This **ideal** assumed that life did not end with death. Instead, death was the beginning of life in a new world.

When a pharaoh died, he left this **realm**. He went to the heavens to join other gods. The pyramid helped him make this journey to the next life. All the **luxuries** from the pharaoh's life on Earth were buried with him. Egyptians believed that a pharaoh would use his possessions in the afterlife.

Making a Mummy

A pharaoh was not buried right after he died. First, his body was carefully prepared for the journey to the next world. This meant he became a mummy! The Egyptians believed that the pharaoh's soul and life force left his body when he died.

Decorated jars held a mummy's vital organs.

However, a pharaoh still needed a body in the next world. The Egyptians figured out a way to protect his body from the **destructive** force of time.

Special priests tended to a pharaoh's body. The work was done under the **leadership** of a priest who wore a jackal mask. This mask was worn because the jackal-faced god Anubis was the god of death and embalming.

All the pharaoh's internal organs, except for the heart, were removed and stored in special jars. Each jar was carved and painted with decorations. The jars would be buried near the pharaoh. What about the heart, though? The heart was the only organ left intact in the body. Egyptians believed that in the afterlife each person's heart would be weighed against a feather. The god Anubis would grant safe **passage** into the afterlife to someone whose heart was light with goodness. Anubis would hand someone whose heart was heavy with wickedness over to a demon.

After most of its organs were removed, the body was stuffed with linen and spices and sewn up. Then, the whole body was covered with a special salt. The body was left like that for 40 days! The salt pulled all the moisture out of the body. Drying a body prevented it from rotting.

The wrappings around this Egyptian mummy have protected it for centuries.

The next step was to wash off the salt. The body was then wrapped in wet linen strips while priests recited prayers of protection. When these strips dried they shrank, tightly **confining** the body in a kind of shell.

Priests also performed a ceremony called the Opening of the Mouth. They didn't really open the pharaoh's mouth, though. Instead they touched sacred objects to his ears, eyes, and mouth. They believed this would allow the pharaoh to hear, see, talk, and eat in the next **realm**. Next, a facemask that **resembled** the pharaoh was placed on the mummy so that he would be recognized in the next world. Facemasks were made of gold and gems, materials worthy of a king.

Then, the mummy was placed inside a coffin. Early coffins were made of reeds or wood and were rectangular. Later, coffins were built of stone shaped more like the human body. The coffins of some mummies were placed inside another coffin or two for extra protection.

After 70 days, the pharaoh was ready for burial. The funeral began. There were thousands of mourners. Yet this was also a happy time. The people celebrated because their pharaoh was on his way to an eternal life. A lot of food and drink were **consumed** at an enormous party.

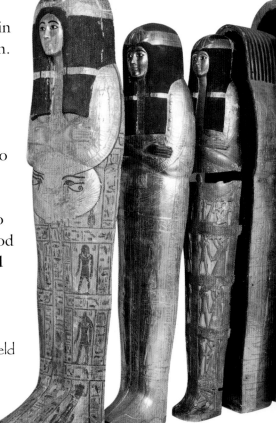

These nested coffins held the mummy of a king.

Treasures for the Afterlife

The early Egyptians were not **reluctant** to die. They believed that Osiris, the god of the underworld, would grant them eternal life. Imagine packing your bags for a vacation that would last forever! That is kind of what a pharaoh did. He was not **confined** to this world. Neither were his worldly goods. He would be surrounded by the same comfort in the afterlife as he had been during his lifetime.

Beds, clothing, and toys were commonly placed near a pharaoh's **tomb**. Fans were included to keep him cool. There might be writing materials and musical instruments. There was jewelry and anything else a pharaoh needed to keep up his appearance, such as combs and jars of lotions. Even food and drink were buried so that the pharaoh could **consume** them in the afterlife.

How could the pharaoh live a **luxurious** afterlife if he had no servants to assist him? The pharaoh had plenty of servants during his earthly life. To provide him with servants during his eternal life, statues of servants were placed in the pyramid. Early Egyptians believed that animals were messengers for the gods. So they made animal mummies, too. They placed them in a pyramid near the pharaoh.

The wealth of **possessions** inside the pyramids made them targets for thieves in later years. Unfortunately, robbers eventually broke into every pyramid. They braved dark, airless, **confining** spaces to steal everything of value.

How is it then that we know so much about the pharaohs? Thieves stole everything that was **movable**, but they could not steal the pyramid itself. The pyramid was **immovable**. Its interior walls were covered in paintings. The walls were also filled with hieroglyphics. That is the written picture language of ancient Egypt. The wall paintings and hieroglyphics remained intact to tell the pharaohs' stories.

9

CHAPTER 3
PYRAMIDS OF ANCIENT EGYPT

Most early Egyptians were buried in a simple hole dug in the desert. The pharaohs received special treatment, however. A pharaoh needed a **tomb** that was both safe and majestic. The king of the **realm** was buried under a mastaba. A mastaba had a rectangular base, sloping sides, and a flat top. It was made out of mud bricks that had been left in the sun to dry.

The pharaoh's burial chamber was located as much as 80 feet below the mastaba. The mastaba was the covering or visual marker for a pharaoh's burial site. It rose out of the desert like a small mound. The Arabic word mastaba means "bench." A bench is what a mastaba might have **resembled**.

Mastabas were certainly noticeable, but they were plain. Around 4,500 years ago, an Egyptian **architect** named Imhotep had a better idea. Imhotep was working in Sakkara on a very large mastaba. It was for the pharaoh, King Dhoser.

One day, Imhotep and his men began to build up instead of building out. They put a second, smaller mastaba on top of the first one. Then, they put a third, even smaller mastaba on top of the second. They built six layers in all. Each layer was slightly smaller than the one below it. The last, top layer came to a point.

Imhotep had just built the first pyramid! This pyramid looked like a giant set of stairs leading to the heavens. That is why it is called the Step Pyramid.

King Dhoser must have been pleased with his Step Pyramid. It was the tallest building in all of Egypt!

The new pyramid rose 200 feet out of the desert. Imagine how impressive this tall structure must have looked to the ancient Egyptians! The Egyptians saw it as the **ideal** burial place for a pharaoh. The pharaoh could use the pyramid like a stairway to climb to the heavens.

Imhotep combined **leadership** and creativity to change the skyline of Egypt forever. He also changed the way pyramids were made. He used stone blocks instead of mud bricks to build the Step Pyramid. This pyramid is the very first building to be made out of stone.

The Step Pyramid still stands at Sakkara today. Wind and desert sandstorms can be very **destructive**, however. The Step Pyramid has lost some of its original height. Imhotep's pyramid is still amazing, though. His creative design set the pattern for many pyramids that followed.

The Step Pyramid changed the world of architecture forever.

The First Smooth-Sided Pyramid

Pharaohs continued to have step pyramids built for many years. Then, the pyramid's shape changed again, during the reign of King Sneferu (2613–2589 BCE). Sneferu was building a step pyramid at Maidum. Then, he moved his whole court to Dashur. The step pyramid at Maidum was abandoned. A new one was started at Dashur.

Was it starting over that gave the builders a new idea? They decided to give the new pyramid smooth outer walls. The sides did not rise step by step. The new pyramid at Dashur became the first one in history with smooth sides. This pyramid was also special in another way. It was bent!

The bottom part of the pyramid slopes inward at an angle of 55 degrees. This angle gets smaller as the pyramid rises. The change in the angle makes the building look wavy or bent. Not surprisingly, it is called the Bent Pyramid. The Bent Pyramid may have an odd shape, but it is still standing strong and **immovable** today!

What did King Sneferu do when he saw his Bent Pyramid? He ordered a whole new pyramid! He wanted one that wasn't bent. The workers started over. This time they succeeded. They built what many people think of as the first true pyramid. The pyramid is tall, straight, and smooth on all sides. It **resembles** the kind of pyramid you probably think of when you think of Egypt. It is called the North Pyramid because it is one mile north of the Bent Pyramid. It is also called the Red Pyramid because of the reddish limestone used to build its interior.

King Sneferu probably didn't mind losing his stairway to heaven. The early Egyptians had a sacred, pointed stone called a benben. It symbolized the sun's rays. The North Pyramid looked like a benben. The pyramid's shape connected it to Ra, the sun god.

The Pyramids of Giza

The North Pyramid was the beginning of a time called The Age of Pyramids. Three pyramids built during this time still tower over the sands of Giza. They are solid and **immovable** monuments. They honor a family whose **leadership** lasted for almost a century. The Great Pyramid is the oldest pyramid of the three. It is also the world's tallest pyramid at 481 feet high. It was built for King Sneferu's son, King Khufu, around 2589 BCE.

The second pyramid was built for Khufu's son, King Khafre. His pyramid is just nine feet shorter than his father's. A huge stone sculpture of a lion with the head of a king sits in front of Khafre's pyramid. The sculpture is known as the Sphinx. The third pyramid was built for Khafre's son, King Menkaure. Menkaure's pyramid is less than half the height of the other two pyramids.

The Pyramids at Giza were built along the west bank of the Nile River. In fact, all Egyptian pyramids were built on the west bank. The river's west side was a symbol of death because every night Ra disappeared in the west. That was why **tombs** were built on the west side of the river. People lived on the river's east side. The river's east side was a symbol of life because the sun god Ra rose each morning in the east.

Time and **tomb** robbers have damaged many of the pyramids. Fortunately, archaeologists have reconstructed what the interior of many pyramids was like. Each pyramid has an entrance leading to a **passageway** that usually slopes down to a storage room.

The storage room held the pharaoh's **luxuries**. It also held the food that the Egyptians thought the pharaoh **consumed** in the afterlife. The next room was the pharaoh's burial chamber. His final resting place was always in the exact center of the pyramid, directly below the pyramid's tip.

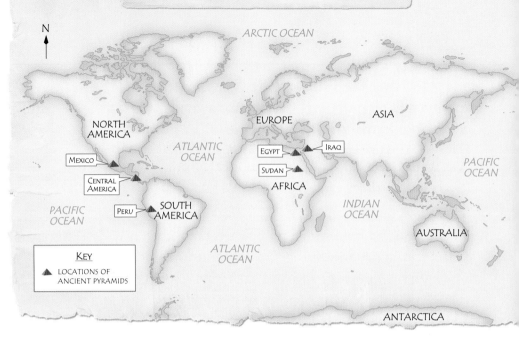

The Great Pyramid's interior was more complex than most pyramids. It had narrow, **confining** corridors leading both up and down. The corridor or **passageway** that went up led to Khufu's burial chamber. It also led to an unfinished chamber called the Queen's Chamber. Many experts believe this chamber was originally intended for Khufu's tomb. They think workers abandoned the chamber when they realized it would be too small. The corridor that sloped down led to an unfinished chamber more than 60 feet below the base of the pyramid.

The Pyramids of Giza were one of the Seven Wonders of the Ancient World. The ancient Greeks and Romans may have marveled at the size of the pyramids. They may have been awed also by the amount of labor and the mathematical precision **involved** in building the pyramids. The Pyramids of Giza are the only Wonder of the Ancient World that is still standing today. That fact alone makes them awesome!

The Pyramid Complex

The pyramids at Giza were not the only buildings at the site. Each pyramid was part of its own "pyramid complex." A pyramid complex included several buildings and other objects. The main and largest building in the complex was always the pyramid.

The building farthest away from the pyramid was the Valley Temple. This building was located on the bank of the Nile. It was where boats arrived with building materials. The pharaoh's body also would eventually arrive there by boat.

A causeway, or roadway, connected the Valley Temple to the rest of the complex. The pharaoh's body would be taken down the causeway to the Mortuary Temple. The Mortuary Temple was right next to the pyramid. In this temple, priests prepared the pharaoh's body for burial.

Large boats were actually buried in boat pits dug around the Mortuary Temple. Why did the Egyptians bury boats? They were the main means of transportation for early Egyptians. Boats made everything **movable**. Egyptians believed that the boats would carry the pharaoh and his **possessions** to the next world.

A number of much smaller pyramids, mastabas, and other burial places were **confined** within each pyramid complex. These burial places were built for people who were important to the pharaoh when he was alive. At the Great Pyramid, three pyramids called the Queens' Pyramids stood to the east of King Khufu's. Mastabas for Khufu's sons and daughters surrounded the Queens' Pyramids.

There were still other people buried on the west side of Khufu's pyramid. Among them was the master builder of the Great Pyramid. A master builder was an important **professional**. A master builder was worthy of the honor of being buried near a pharaoh.

CHAPTER 4
HOW DID THEY BUILD THAT?

Here's a remarkable fact. The Great Pyramid was the tallest building in the world from 2589 BCE until 1887 CE. That's almost 4,000 years! Finally, in 1887 the Eiffel Tower was built in Paris, France. It is 984 feet high, more than twice as tall as the Great Pyramid.

It is truly amazing that for so many years no other building was taller than the Great Pyramid. Just think about it. The workers who built the pyramids of Egypt didn't **possess** any fancy tools. By the time the Eiffel Tower was built, technology had made huge advances. Machines and tools made building much easier. There were even different materials to use, such as steel beams.

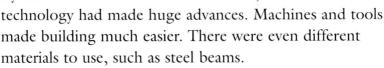

An Egyptian adze

It's easy to see why the Great Pyramid is considered a wonder of the ancient world. It was built of heavy blocks using only the simplest of tools. It took thousands of workers about 20 years to build. Its square base covers more than 13 acres. That's about the size of 10 football fields!

About 2,300,000 blocks were used to build the Great Pyramid. Each block weighed at least 2.5 tons. Think about carrying even one of those!

There's another marvel to consider. Every pyramid lines up with the main points of a compass. Yet, the early Egyptians didn't have compasses. Still, they lined up every pyramid to face exactly north, south, east, and west. How did they manage that? Pyramid builders used the stars to find true north. It is amazing that they were always accurate in lining up the pyramids to face the four compass points.

What basic building tools were used by the early Egyptians? The builders used an adze to chop and shape wood. An adze is a tool with a thin, curved blade. They used chisels and saws to chip or cut stones. They also used mallets and stone balls to shape stones. All these tools were handmade out of copper, wood, or stone.

Workers used these simple tools to get precise results. You might think structures built with these tools would not last long. Yet the pyramids are still strong and **immovable** after thousands of years.

The Egyptian builders also used common sense. To find out where a foundation was uneven, they dug trenches and filled them with water. They also built the underground rooms and **passages** first. Then, they built the pyramid above them. Tunneling down before building up simply made sense.

An Egyptian mallet

The Egyptians used basic handmade tools to build the pyramids.

Masterful Building Methods

How would you move a stone block that weighs 5,000 pounds? That's no easy task, even today. The Egyptian builders knew, however, that rolling objects tend to keep on rolling. They used this fact to find a method to move the big blocks. Their method **involved** pulling the blocks over wooden rollers. This was much easier than dragging the blocks over the sand.

Workers chipped each huge stone block out of a local quarry. To move a block, they placed a pathway of wooden rollers in the sand. Then, they wet the rollers with mud and water so that they would turn in place. Next, the workers tied ropes around a block and hauled it onto the rollers. The rollers were like a conveyer belt. They turned easily as workers pulled the block onto a waiting boat.

The stone blocks floated on the Nile to a building site. Then, they were hauled out of the boat. Again, workers moved each block over a pathway of rollers to the pyramid site. Workers smoothed the block and then put it in place.

No one really knows how the Egyptians got the huge blocks up the sides of a pyramid. Most experts think that the pyramid builders used ramps and pulled the blocks up the ramps on rollers. Many experts think the builders used a single, straight ramp that grew as the pyramid grew. Other experts think there were two ramps. Still others think there was one ramp that curved around the sides of the pyramid, like a road carved into the sides of a steep mountain.

The pyramids built during the Age of Pyramids had a core made of reddish, local limestone. The outer surfaces were made of better-quality, white limestone. Some experts think the surface stone was laid after the entire core was built. Others think the outer stone was laid as the core was being built.

Did the builders take the building ramp down in stages or all at once? The Egyptians may have built the entire core of a pyramid first. Then, they may have laid the surface limestone from the top on down. That would mean they took the ramp down in stages. However, the builders may have laid the surface stones as they built a pyramid's core. That would mean they took the entire ramp down only after the top of a pyramid was completed.

One thing is certain. Pyramids built after the Age of Pyramids were not as sturdy. They were often made of mud bricks. Mud bricks do not last as long as solid stone blocks. Only the ruins of mud-brick pyramids remain today.

The ancient Egyptians labored long and hard to build their amazing pyramids. Read on to learn about other ancient cultures that were inspired by the shape of the pyramid. As you'll see, these cultures also used the pyramid to express important cultural **ideals**.

The Egyptians may have used a system of ramps to build the pyramids.

CHAPTER 5
A LONG WAY FROM EGYPT

Other pyramids were constructed centuries after the last Egyptian pyramid was built. Beginning around 150 CE, pyramids were built halfway around the world from Egypt. It is unlikely that the **architects** of these newer pyramids knew about the long-standing pyramids in other parts of the world. In 150 CE, there were no telephones, television, global mail delivery, or World Wide Web. Travel was difficult, if not impossible. It wasn't until the 1500s that European explorers discovered Mesoamerica.

Mesoamerica is where Mexico and other Latin American countries exist today. It was populated by several different cultures. The Maya and Aztec peoples are probably the best-known native peoples of Mesoamerica.

Mesoamericans were amazing builders and planners. They built advanced cities. Pyramids were the most important buildings in those cities. The pyramids were tall, steep, four-sided structures. They were built in steps. In fact, they **resemble** the Egyptian Step Pyramid.

Staircases were built into the sides of Mesoamerican pyramids so that people could climb to the top. The tops of Mesoamerican pyramids were not pointed like Egyptian pyramids. Instead, low, square buildings were built on top. The buildings were temples used to honor gods.

Some of the Mesoamerican pyramids had temples inside as well. Some had **tombs** beneath them. Warriors sometimes used pyramids almost like a fort to defend their city. However, a pyramid's main purpose was to honor the gods.

Mesoamericans had many gods. The sun god may have been the most important. Mesoamericans believed that each night the sun god turned into the jaguar god of the underworld. The jaguar's spots represented the stars.

A view of the Pyramid of the Sun at Teotihuacán

The Pyramids of Teotihuacán

Teotihuacán was an ancient Mesoamerican city. It was located about 25 miles northeast of where Mexico City, Mexico, is today. Teotihuacán was the first true city in this part of the world. It covered 8 square miles. Pyramids, palaces, marketplaces, and even apartments were built within the city's **confines**. More than 100,000 people lived in Teotihuacán. That is a lot of people for such an ancient city!

The Pyramid of the Sun is the largest pyramid in Teotihuacán. It is also the largest pyramid outside of Egypt. The base of the Pyramid of the Sun is 730 feet on each side. Its base is almost as large as that of the Great Pyramid at Giza. However, the Pyramid of the Sun is much shorter. It is only 200 feet tall.

The Pyramid of the Sun is still very impressive, though. It took 2.5 million tons of stone to build the pyramid. What tools did the Mesoamericans use to build this huge structure? Like the early Egyptians, Mesoamericans only had handmade tools that were made of stone. Workers used the stone tools to chip away at rocks and stones.

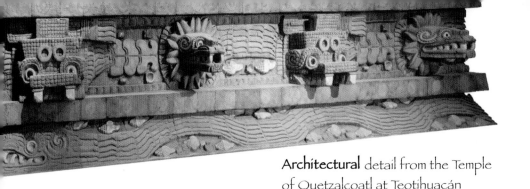

Architectural detail from the Temple
of Quetzalcoatl at Teotihuacán

The core of the Pyramid of the Sun is mostly made up
of packed rubble. Its surface is made of adobe bricks. Adobe
bricks are made of a mixture of mud and straw. The bricks are
formed and left to dry and harden in the sun. The Pyramid
of the Sun has no **passageways**. It also doesn't have any
chambers full of **luxuries**. The pyramid is just a base for the
temple on top. Only priests were allowed in the temple.

Like the Egyptians, the Mesoamericans believed in life
after death. Important people were buried in **tombs**. As
you've read, tombs were sometimes built below Mesoamerican
pyramids. For example, a tomb has been found in a natural
cave located under the Pyramid of the Sun.

There are many possible reasons why the Pyramid of
the Sun was built over a cave. Caves were important in
Mesoamerican culture. They were considered sacred places.
They were seen as the dwelling places of gods and ancestors.
Caves also provided a **passageway** to the underworld. They
were thought of as the source of all creation.

The second tallest pyramid in Teotihuacán is the Pyramid
of the Moon. The Mesoamericans believed that gods were
involved in all parts of nature. They also believed in balancing
what they saw as opposing forces of nature. Therefore, the
Mesoamericans needed to balance the Pyramid of the Sun by
building a pyramid to honor the moon.

Teotihuacán means "Place of the Gods." No one knows
who really built it. When invading Spaniards asked about the
city, the Aztecs said the gods built Teotihuacán.

Maya Pyramids

The Maya people lived in many cities throughout Mesoamerica. They did not have a central **leadership**. Instead, each city had a ruler. Each city also had pyramids. Most of the pyramids were built between the third and ninth century CE.

Maya pyramids were built with heavy stone blocks. The blocks were held together with lime mortar. New pyramids were usually built up around the outside of older pyramids. An older pyramid formed a very sturdy core for a new pyramid. Chambers were built inside the pyramids. Priests would perform secret ceremonies there. The priesthood was an important **profession** in Maya culture.

Maya priests also performed public rituals to please their gods and keep them alive. The Maya believed that in order to stay alive the gods needed human blood! People were not **reluctant** to give their blood to the gods. They considered it an honor.

People would give their blood to the priests. The priests would then offer it to the gods. The Maya believed that their blood sacrifices kept the gods alive. In return, the gods would grant the people a good harvest.

Often, though, blood sacrifices were not enough to satisfy the gods. Sometimes the priests felt that an entire human needed to be sacrificed. Many people were actually put to death for this reason. These human sacrifices took place at the Maya pyramids.

Most sacrificial victims were prisoners of war. The city's men, women, and children might be sacrificed as well. Four people would hold a victim face up on an altar. Then, a priest would cut out the victim's beating heart! The blood from the heart was the most valuable offering to the gods.

Tikal, in Guatemala, was the largest Maya city. It covered more than 6 square miles. About 25,000 people may have lived there. The city contained more than 3,000 buildings, including several pyramid temples. The most famous Tikal pyramid is the Temple of the Giant Jaguar. It has several stepped terraces and is more than 230 feet high. A chamber sits at the top of the pyramid. The chamber was designed to carry the priest's voice to the crowds below.

The Maya also built pyramids in the city of Chichén Itzá. Chichén Itzá is located in present-day Yucatán, Mexico. The Temple of Kukulcán is the most famous pyramid in Chichén Itzá. Kukulcán was the Maya version of Quetzalcoatl, another powerful Mesoamerican god. He was often shown as a feathered serpent with a human head coming out of his mouth. The Temple of Kukulcán rises 75 feet high. This temple also has an inner chamber with a jaguar throne.

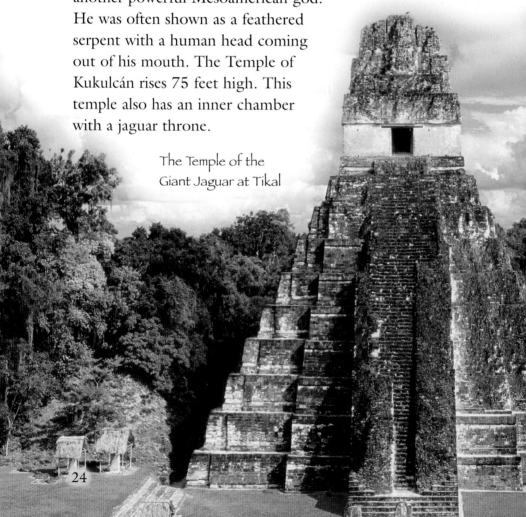

The Temple of the Giant Jaguar at Tikal

Aztec Pyramids

The Aztec people were the last great culture of Mesoamerica. They built a big city not far from Teotihuacán. Their city, Tenochtitlán, was built where Mexico City is located today. It thrived until Spaniards conquered it in the early 1500s.

The Aztecs built many pyramids in their capital city. They used adobe bricks to form a pyramid's core. The surface was made of stone bricks held together by mortar. The tallest pyramid was about 95 feet high. It was called the Great Temple. Like other Mesoamerican pyramids, the Great Temple was very steep. It had stone stairways leading up to the top. However, there were two temples—not one—on top of the pyramid at Tenochtitlán.

One temple was dedicated to the god of rain and one to the god of war. These gods controlled the harvest. Healthy crops require a lot of rain, but what did war have to do with a good harvest? The Aztec people believed they needed to give the gods a lot of human blood in order to receive a good harvest. The Aztec **leadership** started many wars in order to provide a steady supply of captives. These captives became **reluctant** victims of sacrifices.

Warriors were important **professionals** in Aztec society because they supplied the victims of sacrifice. The priests sacrificed the prisoners of war brought to them by the warriors. The Aztecs did more than just cut out the victim's heart. They also **consumed** the person's flesh! The Aztecs believed this brought them closer to their gods.

It's possible their pyramids also allowed the Mesoamericans to feel closer to their gods. The pyramids gave the gods a special place that was high up and apart from everyday life. Perhaps the Mesoamericans' reasons for building pyramids weren't all that different from the Egyptians' reasons.

CHAPTER 6
ZIGGURATS–DWELLING PLACES OF THE GODS

The Mesoamericans were not the first to build pyramids. They were also not the first to create cities. That happened centuries earlier in a place called Mesopotamia. Mesopotamia was located between the Tigris and Euphrates rivers where Iraq is today. In fact, Mesopotamia means "the land between two rivers."

From 3500 BCE until 500 BCE, several different, powerful cultures rose and fell in this region. The Sumerian, Babylonian, and Assyrian peoples are the best known. These Mesopotamians all built cities. They also built structures that **resembled** pyramids. These structures are called ziggurats. The word *ziggurat* means "to build high."

Every city had a ziggurat. Some had more than one. Ziggurats were the tallest buildings in cities. A ziggurat was part of a temple complex. The tower-like ziggurat was usually built next to a temple that was at ground level. Ziggurats were believed to be dwelling places for the gods. Mesopotamians also saw ziggurats as places where they could get close to an **ideal** by being close to a god.

As in early Egypt and Mesoamerica, gods were very important in Mesopotamia. People believed that the gods lived on mountaintops. Ziggurats were actually built to **resemble** mountains. They were designed to be a place in a city where gods would feel at home.

Almost 30 ziggurats have been discovered. They are all in various phases of **destruction**. Experts believe that each ziggurat originally had a temple at its top. None of these temples exist any longer. Stairways are still intact on the sides of some ziggurats, however. These stairways support the belief that temples once existed at the top of ziggurats.

Every ziggurat had at least one stairway on one of its sides. Most ziggurats had either three or seven stepped levels. Each level was painted a different color. From a distance people could see layers of bright colors. The colors had special meanings, but experts do not agree about what the colors meant. What we do know is that a ziggurat would be hard to miss!

Here's something else to consider. In all of Mesopotamia, there were no forests and no stones! **Architects** didn't have any wood or rocks to build with. Instead, they made bricks out of mud and reeds. These bricks were very similar to the adobe bricks used by the Mesoamericans. Not all the Mesopotamian bricks were sun-dried, however. The surface of a ziggurat was made of glazed bricks that had been baked in a type of kiln, or oven. These oven-baked bricks were much harder and stronger than bricks dried in the sun.

Small statues from a Sumerian temple

Steep steps lead to the top of this ziggurat.

Kings ruled Mesopotamia. King Ur-Nammu ruled from 2112 to 2004 BCE. He had a ziggurat built in Ur to honor the moon god Nanna. The ziggurat at Ur is the best-preserved ziggurat found so far.

The ziggurat at Ur originally had three levels. It was 70 feet high when new. The ziggurat has been worn away by weather and time, however. Only one level remains intact. A great staircase on the northern side of the ziggurat also survives intact.

Mesopotamian **architects** built ziggurats according to the four compass directions. Ziggurats lined up exactly north, south, east, and west. The Mesopotamians must have used the stars to guide their directions, just as the Egyptians did.

Etemenanki is the name of the largest ziggurat found so far. Etemananki is a Sumerian word. It means "foundation of heaven and earth." Etemananki was built in the city of Babylon, near present-day Baghdad, Iraq. This ziggurat was begun during the reign of the Babylonian king Hammurabi (1792–1750 BCE). It was completed much later during the reign of Nebuchadnezzar II (604–562 BCE). It had seven levels and was 300 feet tall. Today, Babylon and Etemenanki are mostly in ruins.

Nowadays we are used to seeing city skylines that are full of tall skyscrapers. At the time ziggurats were built, most buildings were low to the ground. It must have been an amazing sight to see the brightly colored ziggurats towering over Mesopotamian cities. The ziggurats once pointed toward the heavens. We can also see them as monuments that pointed out what people can accomplish.

A model of a ziggurat

CHAPTER 7
PYRAMIDS OF KUSH

Pyramids were built in different places. They were built at different times. People from several different cultures were **involved** in building them. Yet all pyramids look somewhat alike. They were even built to express similar **ideals**.

This statue shows a Kushite king offering a gift to the falcon god Hemen.

At least one culture based its pyramids on those of ancient Egypt. The ancient Kushite people of southern Nubia built many pyramids that were influenced by the Egyptians. The kingdom of Kush was located south of Egypt, where Sudan is located today.

The Kushites developed a complex culture. They established the oldest African city found outside of Egypt. At times, they controlled trade between Central Africa and Egypt. They created large temples dedicated to their gods.

The ancient Kushites and Egyptians knew one another for centuries. They were trading partners, but they were not friendly neighbors. They engaged in many battles. Egypt occupied and controlled Kush for several centuries. Kush in turn occupied and controlled Egypt for almost a century.

Kushite kings began building pyramids around 747 BCE. By then the Egyptians had stopped building them. In the end, the Kushites actually built more pyramids than the Egyptians did. More than 200 Kushite pyramids have been found.

Like the Egyptians, the Kushites believed their kings were gods on Earth. Their kings were the sons of the Kushite sun god, Amun-Pa. Kushites saw pyramids as symbols of the rising sun. The Kushites also believed in an afterlife. They believed a pyramid helped their king return to the gods after his death.

29

Kushite pyramids are not as grand as the Egyptian pyramids. They have much smaller bases and much steeper sides. They are flat at the very top, rather than pointed.

A Kushite pyramid had three main parts. The first was the royal **tomb** under the pyramid. As in Egypt, Kushite kings were buried with many **possessions**, including statues of servants. When the king entered the afterlife, these statues were supposed to come alive to take care of him.

The pyramid itself was the second part of the overall structure. It symbolized a stairway to the heavens. A small chapel on the pyramid's eastern side was the third part. People placed offerings to the dead king there.

The Kushites built their pyramids on the Nile River's west side, just as the Egyptians had. The first Kushite pyramids were built at a place called el-Kurru. The site of el-Kurru became a royal cemetery. Several generations of kings and queens were buried under the pyramids at el-Kurru. In fact, kings and queens who had originally been buried elsewhere were later moved to el-Kurru. Nuri and Meroë are two other royal burial sites where pyramids were built.

What similar **ideals** did the Kushites and Egyptians have? They both believed their kings were gods in human form. Both peoples also believed their kings descended from the all-important sun god. In both cultures, the distinct shape of pyramids stood out against the desert sky. For both peoples, this shape was symbolic of the sun. It even looked like a stairway to the heavens where the sun lived.

A Kushite pyramid

Does it make sense that these two peoples developed similar **ideals** and ways of expressing them? The early Egyptians and the Kushites lived at the same time and very near one another. They were trading partners for many centuries. At times they were enemies, but they still had many opportunities to borrow ideas from one other.

It makes sense that Kushites built pyramids like their Egyptian neighbors. How do you explain the pyramids of Mesopotamia, however? How do you explain the Mesoamerican pyramids? These cultures didn't exist near the Egyptians or the Kushites. It is unlikely that they were even aware of Egypt or Kush. Mesoamerica is halfway around the world from Egypt and Kush. Yet Mesoamerican cultures also built pyramids to honor gods and placed tombs below the pyramids. The sun god was important in Mesoamerican cultures as well.

There are even more similarities among these ancient cultures. In all of them, priests and warriors were important **professionals**. These cultures were all dependent on good harvests. Perhaps concern about harvests was a major force behind their religious beliefs. We can find many common

A royal crown from Kush

threads among these ancient cultures. We can't fully explain why they **resembled** one another so strongly, however.

Will the mystery of the pyramid's widespread importance ever be fully solved? It is impossible to predict. We have yet to discover all the world's pyramids. As each new pyramid is found, we learn more about how people lived long ago. Perhaps the greatest thing the pyramids will teach us is that people were—and are— not so different from one another after all. That's a pretty amazing idea in itself!

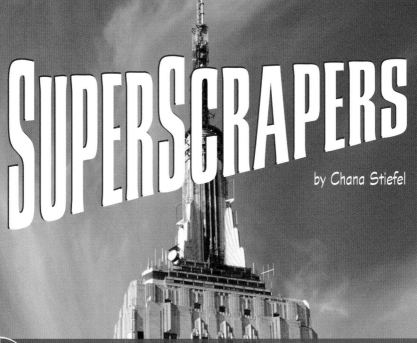

SUPERSCRAPERS

by Chana Stiefel

Chapter 1

Super Tall

Suppose you're standing on top of the Empire State Building. New York City's busy streets are 86 floors below you. Cars and buses look like toys. Above you, there's nothing but crystal-clear, blue sky.

You can see as far as 80 miles in every direction. On the horizon you can spot New Jersey, Pennsylvania, Connecticut, even Massachusetts! To the south stands the Statue of Liberty. She holds her torch **prominently** above New York Harbor.

In fact, you are up so high, you start to feel a little dizzy…and a little scared! You start to wonder: Why would someone construct such a tall building in the first place?

Throughout history, people have tried to build tall buildings. Some of the earliest were **meaningful** symbols. The Great Pyramid of Giza is Egypt's tallest pyramid. When it was completed 4,600 years ago, the pyramid rose more than 480 feet. That's nearly 50 stories high.

Tall structures were built as symbols of power in the Middle Ages. Chartres is a cathedral. It was completed in France in 1220 CE. It represented the power of the Catholic Church. The massive cathedral has more than 150 stained-glass windows. Chartres's tallest spire rises 378 feet. The cathedral inspired awe in its worshippers. It was also built to make other churches look puny!

Not all tall buildings were built to inspire awe. Sometimes people **utilized** tall towers for protection. In the Middle Ages, San Gimignano was a wealthy town in Italy. A protective wall surrounded it. In the 1200s, two **prominent** families fought each other for control of the town. One family won and chased the other out. The winning family was concerned. They thought that the losers might try to fight back. For protection, they built a new tower to live in. The losing family tried to invade the town. People in the tower were ready for them. They shot arrows and threw down garbage on the losers. They even poured boiling water on them to chase them away.

Back then, a tower represented a family's great wealth. The higher the tower, the richer and more important a family was. The inhabitants of San Gimignano built a total of 72 towers. Fifteen of them still stand today.

By the late 1800s, people were erecting tall buildings for another reason. Cities were becoming too crowded. Low buildings were pressed together like books on a shelf. There was no land left. Yet cities needed more buildings. The only place to go was up.

New York City has the Empire State Building, so you might think it's the place where skyscrapers got their start. However, the real birthplace of the skyscraper is 718 miles west of New York City—in Chicago, Illinois.

34

Reaching for the Sky

What makes a building a skyscraper? A skyscraper is an extremely tall building. Would a pyramid or a cathedral be considered a skyscraper by today's standards? No. They are tall, and they are **meaningful** buildings. Yet they're not tall enough to be considered skyscrapers. The age of the skyscraper did not begin until the late nineteenth century in Chicago.

On the night of October 8, 1871, in a Chicago suburb, flames erupted in a barn belonging to the O'Leary family. According to legend, a cow kicked over a **portable** oil lamp. The burning oil sparked the blaze. Strong winds whipped up the flames. The raging inferno had leaped over two rivers by midnight. Chicago's business district caught fire. The blaze continued to torch the city throughout the following day. Finally, rain helped extinguish the flames.

Historians called it the Great Chicago Fire. It burned an area of land 4 miles long and about three-quarters of a mile wide. As many as 18,000 buildings—roughly a third of the city—burned to the ground. Three hundred people lost their lives. More than 90,000 people were left homeless.

Rather than abandon their beloved city, the people used their **resolve** to rebuild it. Within 6 weeks of the fire, more than 300 new buildings were under construction. Chicago was determined to reestablish itself as one of the great cities of the United States. During the rebuilding, thousands of people went there to find jobs. Between 1880 and 1890, the population doubled. Real-estate prices skyrocketed. One area of town filled with small businesses. Because of the rising cost of real estate and the fast-growing population, the best way to rebuild was to reach for the sky.

Colored lights at the top of the Empire State Building change to reflect national holidays. What holiday do you think the red, white, and blue lights signify?

From Stone to Steel

Developers in Chicago were determined to make the city taller and safer. They knew they had to **modify** their old construction techniques to do this. They had to use new materials. Most tall buildings at the time were constructed using masonry. Masonry **consists** of stone blocks. The blocks are cemented on top of one another. What's wrong with that? Well, nothing, if you want a short building.

Masonry buildings can only climb four or five stories high. Why? The stone blocks in the walls are very strong. Yet they are also very heavy. The masonry walls are called load-bearing walls. These walls support the weight of the building. Here is the problem. The stones at the bottom of a building must be thick enough to support the weight of everything on top of them. The taller a building gets, the heavier the walls become. In turn, the stones in the lower walls must be built thicker and thicker to support more weight. The thicker the walls are, the less room there is for people.

Masonry buildings are also very dark. Adding large windows weakens the building's outer walls, so masonry buildings have fewer and smaller windows. Some masonry buildings in the 1800s **utilized** iron beams for extra support. However, the Great Chicago Fire showed that iron melts under intense heat. Builders had to find new ways to deal with these problems.

Fortunately, inventors had new ideas on how to build better buildings. Perhaps the most **essential** new idea was to use steel. Steel is a strong, hard material that **consists** of iron and other metals that can be easily shaped. Steel is stronger than iron and also more fire-resistant. By the late 1800s, steel had been used for bridges, but not buildings. That was about to change, thanks to a man and his pet bird's cage.

William Le Baron Jenney was a structural engineer. He lived in Chicago. A structural engineer uses science and math to design buildings. Jenney was working on the design for the Home Insurance Company's new Chicago headquarters.

As legend has it, Jenney left work one day feeling sick. He went home. At home, Jenney watched his wife pick up a heavy book. She placed it on top of a wire birdcage. That gave Jenney an idea! If the thin metal wire of the birdcage could support a heavy book, why couldn't steel beams hold up an entire building?

Jenney's new idea was called steel-frame, or skeletal, construction. **Essentially**, the steel skeleton in his building worked like a birdcage. The steel beams also worked like the bones in the human body. Human skin doesn't support the body's weight. It just hangs on the outside of the body. A bony skeleton supports the human body **internally**. In a similar manner, the steel skeleton of a building holds the building up. The walls just hang on the sides, like skin.

The outside walls of his steel-frame building weren't called skin, though. They were called curtain walls. They hung on the outside like curtains. Unlike masonry walls, they were equally thin from top to bottom. Curtain walls allowed more room for office space on every floor. The walls could also be filled with windows. More windows would allow more sunlight into the building.

Jenney's Home Insurance Building was completed in 1885. It is considered the world's first skyscraper. Yet it was only 10 stories high. Today's superscrapers are ten times that height! Back then, though, people thought a 10-story building was extremely tall. They worried about the building's safety because it was so tall. Construction was briefly stopped. People had to be convinced the building wouldn't fall down!

In less than ten years, dozens of skyscrapers were built all over downtown Chicago. The buildings cast long, dark shadows. People were concerned that the streets would become dark canyons. In 1893, the city decided to **restrict** the height of new buildings. They could be no taller than 10 stories.

New York City, however, had no such height **restrictions**. A 22-story building was built in 1902. It was shaped like a triangle. It was called the Fuller Building, but it became better known as the Flatiron Building because from the top, it looks like an old-fashioned iron. That's how it got that name. It was built using a steel frame. After seeing this building go up, big companies all around the city wanted their own skyscrapers.

Why would a company want to own a skyscraper? Big companies realized that building a skyscraper with their name on it was a great way to advertise. They could also make extra money by renting out office space in their huge buildings. In 1908, the 41-story, 612-foot Singer Building broke all records for height. It was named for a sewing machine manufacturer. That record fell to the 700-foot Metropolitan Life Tower in 1909 and then the 792-foot Woolworth Building in 1913. Each new building was taller than the last. Yet the real race for the sky was just about to begin.

Chapter 3

Dueling Skyscrapers

Have you ever wanted to win something badly? Maybe you were playing a video game. Maybe you were playing basketball. Well, in the late 1920s, Craig Severance and William Van Alen were bitter rivals. They were architects. Both men wanted to build the world's tallest building. The two had been partners. They built shops, banks, hotels, and restaurants together. Van Alen was very creative. Severance was a good businessman. However, **internal** conflicts caused their partnership to break up.

In November 1928, car manufacturer Walter Chrysler hired Van Alen to design a magnificent skyscraper on Forty-second Street in New York City. Chrysler wanted the building to be a **meaningful** symbol of his company's success. Van Alen wanted the building to be a skyscraper like no one had ever seen. For four months, Van Alen worked hard **modifying** his plans. On March 7, 1929, Chrysler showed Van Alen's design to the world. By the following spring, the 809-foot, 68-story tower would be the tallest building in the world.

Van Alen's success made Severance jealous. Then, a businessman named George Ohrstrom hired Severance to design a building for the Bank of Manhattan Company. On April 10, 1929, they announced that their 67-story building would be even taller than Chrysler's. It would be a record-breaking 857 feet! At $20 million, it would cost $5 million more than Chrysler's building. It would be completed at the same time, and it would be taller!

Chrysler fought back. He ordered Van Alen to add floors to his building to make sure it was taller! He didn't care how much it cost. The race was officially on.

The Home Insurance Building in Chicago is considered to be the world's first skyscraper.

Higher!

Chrysler told Van Alen that he could **modify** the design however he wanted. There was only one catch. They would have to keep their design plans secret. This was one competition they could not lose.

Van Alen got right to work. He **resolved** to add floors to the pointed dome. That would bring the height to 77 stories. Six semicircular arches of gleaming steel would point toward the sky on each side of the dome. Triangular-shaped windows—like upside-down Vs for Van Alen—would decorate the arches. However, the building would be about 860 feet. That was almost exactly as tall as Severance's building. That was still **inadequate**. Van Alen needed more height. He had to be sure.

At the same time, Severance was hard at work on his building. Construction crews had built most of his building's **foundation** by the end of May 1929. Yet steelwork of Van Alen's building had already risen to the fourteenth floor. With his eye on a May 1, 1930, deadline, Severance wanted to reach the finish line first. No one had ever built a building so tall and so fast.

Then, somehow, Severance got wind of Van Alen's plans! In August 1929, Severance added 5 penthouse floors to his original 67 stories. He also decided to fasten a 25-foot flagpole to top off the building. Its final height would be 925 feet, much taller than the Chrysler Building. He, too, would **resolve** to keep his plans top secret.

On October 18, 1929, the buildings were only **partially** completed. Yet a newspaper ran this headline: "New Skyscraper Race Is Won by Bank of Manhattan Building." The report was premature, but it made Severance **progressively** more confident. He began to relax and celebrate. He didn't know about Van Alen's last-minute surprise.

In the last week of November, newspapers reported that Van Alen had secretly ordered workers to assemble the **portable** sections of a 185-foot steel spire. They were building it *inside* the dome of the building itself. No one could see what the workers were doing. One day without warning, the spire pierced through the roof like a needle. The spire made the Chrysler Building 1,046 feet tall. It was the tallest building in the world!

For Severance the news was like a needle in his heart. He had completed his building in record time. Yet no one cared. He pointed out that the Bank of Manhattan Building had 70 "usable" stories, so it was better! The Chrysler Building had only 68 usable stories. Unfortunately for him, people only cared about which building was taller.

Van Alen and Chrysler didn't get to brag for too long. Their building would hold the record for only 1 year. Construction of another skyscraper ten blocks away had already started. When completed, this skyscraper would be 204 feet taller than the Chrysler Building. It would quickly become the most famous skyscraper in the world.

The bold outlines and strong geometric forms featured on the Chrysler Building are typical of a design style known as Art Deco.

The Eighth Wonder of the World

Craig Severance and William Van Alen weren't the only men in New York building skyscrapers. John Raskob was an executive at the General Motors car company. Raskob owned 2 acres of land in the middle of the city. Al Smith was the former governor of New York. He was friends with many of the city's powerful politicians. The two worked together to build the city's most **prominent** skyscraper: the Empire State Building. This building would stand more than a quarter-mile high when it was finished.

The question was, how to erect a building that high? The city's building laws said that buildings had to get narrower as they grew taller. That way, they wouldn't block all of the **essential** light from streets below and buildings nearby. This law made it hard for William Lamb to design. He was one of the building's architects. He went through 15 designs. None of them looked right. Then, Lamb held up his pencil. The pencil's clean, straight lines inspired him.

Lamb started to draw. The building had a wide base up to the fifth floor. The rest of the building was narrower. His design allowed the building to rise more than 80 stories straight up. The "pencil point" would **consist** of a 200-foot tower made of glass, aluminum, and steel. The tower would be a perfect crown.

The plans were set. Then, something terrible happened. The stock market crashed in October 1929. Thousands of businesses failed. Millions of people lost their jobs. However, Raskob was able to turn the Great Depression to his advantage. There were so few jobs that people were willing to work long hours for very little money. The cost of materials dropped, too. As a result, the Empire State Building ended up costing $8 million less than its original $50 million budget.

The construction of the Empire State Building was truly amazing. In October 1929, a demolition crew began tearing down the Waldorf-Astoria Hotel, which stood on the site. By January 1930, steam shovels were digging out earth and rock to build the **foundation** that would support the massive tower. Construction of the steel frame began on March 17, 1930.

A crew **consisting** of 4,000 workers labored day and night. The builders wanted to speed up construction. They ordered materials from several different factories. Sixty thousand tons of steel beams arrived from the furnaces of Pittsburgh's steel mills. Some claimed that the beams were still warm! Cement and mortar were shipped from Upstate New York. Some 200,000 cubic feet of Indiana limestone and granite and 10 million bricks were also hauled in. Workers assembled all of these materials at the construction site. It was as if they were putting a giant jigsaw puzzle together.

The building rose at an average rate of 4.5 floors per week. During one 10-day period, the building leaped 14 floors! The builders moved higher and higher with the tower. A minirailroad was built at each level of the tower. It was used to carry supplies back and forth between the construction site and where they kept the supplies. **Portable** cafeterias were set up on five levels. That way, workers wouldn't waste time going down to the street for lunch.

Working on the edge of a steel beam was risky. Wind, rain, heat, and cold added to the danger. However, the heroic "sky boys" who riveted, or fastened, beams together at dizzying heights made it look easy. Nevertheless, a hospital was set up on the ground floor for emergencies. Unfortunately, accidents did happen. Five workers died during the building's construction.

Work on the Empire State Building was often dangerous.

On May 1, 1931, the Empire State Building celebrated its grand opening. It was built in record time—1 year and 45 days. At 1,250 feet, it was the tallest building in the world. It would keep its title for 41 years. Because of the Depression, however, the building had trouble attracting **occupants**. Half of its offices remained empty for 10 years. Some even called it the "Empty State Building." The building didn't fill up until the economic boom that followed World War II.

You can see why the Empire State Building is nicknamed the "Eighth Wonder of the World." Today, 73 elevators whisk people through 7 miles of elevator shafts. They carry some 20,000 people who work for 850 companies with offices in the building.

About 250 people maintain the building. They change the 3,194,547 light bulbs. They plug leaks in 70 miles of water pipes. They oversee 1,060 miles of telephone cable. Some 100 tons of garbage are taken away from the building each month. All New York City television and FM radio stations broadcast from the top of the tower.

On October 23, 1986, the Empire State Building was declared a National Historic Landmark. That means it can never be torn down because it is a valuable part of New York City's history. How valuable? More than 3.5 million tourists visit the Empire State Building every year!

Chapter 4

How Are Skyscrapers Designed and Built?

New kinds of skyscrapers started to rise in cities during the 1960s and 1970s. At first, most of the new office towers were tall, rectangular boxes made of steel, glass, and concrete. Developers didn't care if they looked similar to other skyscrapers. They just had to be tall.

Skyscrapers started to pop up in all sorts of shapes. Chicago's John Hancock Center was built in 1969. Its nickname is Big John. The skyscraper is a huge, square-shaped tube. It gets narrower as it rises. San Francisco's Transamerica Tower was built in 1972. It's a tall, narrow pyramid shape. At first, the pyramid was controversial. Its shape was considered to be very bold. Today, it is the focal point of the city. The Sears Tower in Chicago broke the world record for height in 1974. This building was made up of a bundle of nine tubes. The tubes end at varying heights. The tallest tube reaches 1,454 feet. Atlanta's Peachtree Plaza Hotel was completed in 1976. It looks like a kaleidoscope. It's a tall cylinder with a revolving restaurant on the roof.

These skyscrapers may all look very different. Yet they were all built in much the same way. The leap from an idea in someone's head to a 100-story building is truly amazing. Let's take a look at how it is done.

Sometimes a big company wants to put its main offices in a new building. Of course, just any skyscraper is not **adequate**. The company wants the best! The company also wants to sell or rent office space in the skyscraper to other companies. It will be easier to sell or rent space if the building is really special. To be really special, it might be very tall. It might have an unusual shape, like a pyramid.

Next, the company hires an architect. The architect designs the skyscraper. An architect is a lot like an artist. The architect uses computer programs and draws plans for the building. The plans include drawings of the outside and the inside. They cover everything from offices to elevators to bathrooms.

The architect works closely with engineers. Engineers make sure the architect's ideas actually work. They also design the electrical, heating, cooling, and plumbing systems. Other engineers test the rock and soil of the building site. Thousands of blueprints are drawn and **modified**. The city hires architects and engineers to inspect the blueprints. Once the city says everything looks **adequately** safe, construction can begin.

Constructing a Skyscraper

Architects and engineers plan a skyscraper. Who builds it? That's the job of a contractor. A contractor's crew includes construction workers, crane operators, carpenters, ironworkers, and electricians. The crew uses trucks, cranes, and jackhammers to make it all happen. The building crew has to work as a team. Timing is everything. The longer the construction takes, the more money it costs. Everyone has to be at the right place at the right time. They have to follow the construction plans exactly.

Today, new buildings usually rise on the sites of old buildings. That means the old buildings must be destroyed. To get rid of the old buildings, workers blow them up with dynamite. Then they knock down whatever is left with wrecking cranes. Bulldozers and dump trucks carry away the rubble. Before the Empire State Building was built, 16,000 truckloads of rubble from the Waldorf-Astoria Hotel had to be taken away.

Next comes the **foundation**. It is hidden below ground. A building depends on a strong base to support its weight. Some buildings can weigh more than 300,000 tons! If its base isn't built properly, the building can sink or lean. Italy's famous Tower of Pisa leans so much that it looks as if it's going to fall over!

The best base for a **foundation** is bedrock. Bedrock is the solid rock hidden below layers of soil and clay. To get down to bedrock, workers use explosives and jackhammers. Then, bulldozers and steam shovels scoop rubble onto trucks.

The Sears Tower is nearly the height of 5 football fields standing end to end. Six robots are programmed to clean its 16,100 windows 8 times a year. The tower contains enough concrete to build a 5-mile-long, 8-lane-wide highway.

The type of **foundation** that is used for a building depends on how far the bedrock is beneath the surface. If it is near the surface, workers build footings. Footings are huge concrete slabs that serve as a building's **foundation**. They stand right on the bedrock. The footings for the Empire State Building go down 30 feet below street level. If the bedrock is deeper, workers drive long steel columns called piles hundreds of feet into the ground. They stop when they hit the solid rock.

Next, steel workers attach large vertical steel columns onto their footings. These columns support the skyscraper. Each footing and column must be set perfectly straight. Without solid footings, a column might lean. A leaning column could cause the building to collapse.

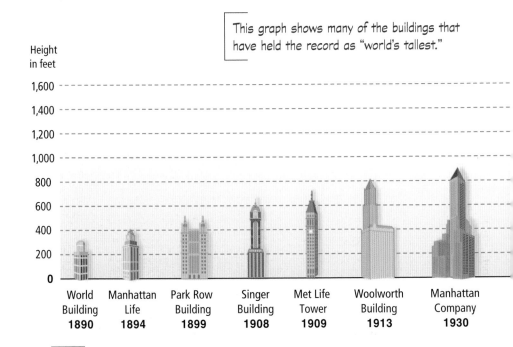

Height in feet

This graph shows many of the buildings that have held the record as "world's tallest."

1,600
1,400
1,200
1,000
800
600
400
200
0

| World Building 1890 | Manhattan Life 1894 | Park Row Building 1899 | Singer Building 1908 | Met Life Tower 1909 | Woolworth Building 1913 | Manhattan Company 1930 |

Superstructures

Once the **foundations** are set, the real work starts. Workers start building the skyscraper's superstructure. The superstructure is everything on a skyscraper that's above the ground. The superstructure is what can set one skyscraper apart from all the others.

The main ingredient of the superstructure is steel, and lots of it. Crane operators at the building site lift one massive steel beam after another off trucks. A powerful jack raises **portable** cranes from floor to floor. These cranes then lift the steel beams higher and higher as the building grows. The ironworkers and welders are like kids on a jungle gym. They climb all over the frame. They bolt and weld the steel beams together. How much steel is used in a skyscraper? Well, the Sears Tower **utilized** 76,000 tons of steel. That's enough metal to build more than 50,000 cars.

How do workers keep track of so much steel? If you've ever built a model plane from a kit, you know that each piece has a letter or number on it. If you match up the letters or numbers in order, you can build your model.

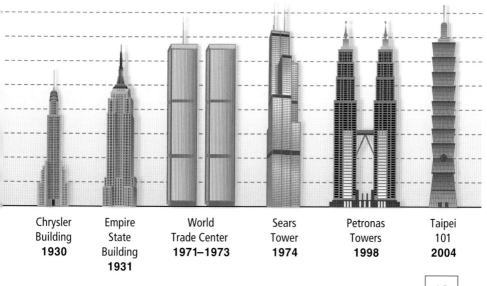

| Chrysler Building **1930** | Empire State Building **1931** | World Trade Center **1971–1973** | Sears Tower **1974** | Petronas Towers **1998** | Taipei 101 **2004** |

Skyscrapers are built the same way. Each piece of steel in the building plan is labeled. The plans show the size, shape, and location of each piece. Once the steel gets to the building site, the workers just put the huge, life-sized "kit" together.

When the highest beam is finally attached, construction workers celebrate. This part of building a skyscraper has a name. It is called topping out. Workers might raise a flag or place a small tree at the top. Their work is still only **partially** complete.

While the superstructure is being built, workers on lower floors are hanging the curtain wall. These outer walls can **consist** of a wide variety of materials. They give each building a unique look. For example, the Sears Tower is enclosed by 16,100 windows and 28 acres of black-coated aluminum. The dark color **lessens** the appearance of city dirt. New York City's Lipstick Building has a glossy red granite covering. This building looks like a giant lipstick tube.

Inside the building, workers are installing the building's "guts." The guts include pipes, electricity, and heating and cooling systems. Norwest Center is a skyscraper in Minneapolis, Minnesota. It contains 30 miles of plumbing pipe and 150 miles of electrical wire. Combined, that's almost enough wire and pipe to stretch from New York to Boston!

A worker wearing safety equipment on a modern skyscraper

Open for Business

Meanwhile, huge concrete mixers start arriving at the site. Their giant drums stir concrete. Concrete is a mixture of sand, gravel, water, and cement. It is very strong. A 33-ton truck could park on a fist-sized chunk of concrete without crushing it.

Big cages called hoists lift workers, tools, and fresh concrete to each level of the skyscraper. The workers fill the steel beams with concrete. The beams are also coated with fireproofing material. Sheets of steel are bolted to each floor. Workers then pour concrete on top of the steel floors.

While the floors are drying, the construction crew works on the building's core. The core acts as the backbone of the building. Just like your backbone, it provides support and helps carry weight. Many skyscraper cores also contain stairs and elevators. Elevators are really important in 100-story buildings! The elevators in Chicago's John Hancock Center travel at 1,801 feet per minute. That's nearly three floors every second.

Next come finishing touches, such as carpet, paint, light fixtures, and doors. The building is almost ready for business. Inspectors have to make sure the work has been done properly and safely. It is **essential** for a building of this size to be safe. It has to be safe for the people who **utilize** it. It also has to be safe for the people on the outside. Nothing can come loose and fall off. Even a penny falling off a skyscraper could hurt someone.

Once inspectors say that the building is okay, the only thing it needs is people. Some skyscrapers hold as many people as a small town. The Sears Tower was designed to hold more than 12,000 **occupants**. In addition, about 25,000 visitors and tourists pass through the building every day.

Chapter 5

Today's Tallest Skyscrapers

Today, almost every city in the world shows off its skyscrapers. New York alone has more than 2,000! Yet, the United States no longer holds the crown for the world's tallest building. In 1996, a country in Asia took the lead for the first time ever. The Sears Tower gave up its title that year to the Petronas Towers in Kuala Lumpur. This city is the capital of Malaysia. The Petronas Towers made this small Indonesian country, located south of Thailand, famous all around the world!

The two towers soar above the city at 1,483 feet. They are 29 feet higher than the Sears Tower. The towers were built by Petronas, the country's oil and gas company. The two 88-story buildings dominate the skyline. Most of the other buildings in the city are hundreds of feet shorter than the towers!

There are lots of remarkable things about the towers besides their height. First, the towers resemble rocket ships. A glass sky bridge connects the two towers at the forty-first and forty-second floors! The bridge was built on the ground. Then it was lifted into place between the towers. It was designed to give **occupants** of the towers an easy way to move between the buildings. It also provides an escape route in case of an emergency.

Can you imagine walking 192 feet from one building to the next, suspended 558 feet in midair? The sky bridge is safe. Yet it still sounds scary! Sometimes wind gusts cause the building to sway. When that happens, the sky bridge is designed to move up and down. You may think that the bridge is going to break when you feel it start to move. Yet the movement is intentional. It helps to **lessen** pressure on the bridge as the buildings move.

Each of the two towers looks round from afar, but the floor plan actually **consists** of two squares. The squares overlap to form eight-pointed stars. Decorative half-circles connect the points of the stars and add more floor space to the design.

The materials are also a little different than those used to build U.S. skyscrapers. These towers do not have a steel frame. Instead, builders **utilized** a frame made of high-strength concrete. The local workers were more used to working with this material. The special concrete also provides more stability in wind than steel does. To **lessen** construction time, a separate building contractor

On a windy day, would you walk on the bridge that connects the Petronas Towers?

was hired for each tower. As many as 1,000 people were working on each tower at the peak of construction. It took a little more than 2 years to build the towers.

The towers now contain a virtual city. There are more than 1.5 million square feet of stores and restaurants, underground parking for 4,500 cars, a museum, an 840-seat concert hall, and a conference center. The building has 32,000 windows. It takes 1 month for window washers to clean each tower just once!

The Petronas Towers held the record as the world's tallest building for only seven years. In October 2003, the title went to an office tower called Taipei 101. This tower is in Taiwan. Taiwan is an island located near the eastern coast of China. Ready for **occupancy** at the end of 2004, the building stands at 1,667 feet. Perhaps its most shocking feature is that it is built in an earthquake zone!

The city of Taipei is tragically familiar with the damage that earthquakes can do. When the building was **partially** finished in March 2002, a quake measuring 6.8 on the Richter scale shook the tower. The tremors threw two cranes, steel beams, and chunks of cement crashing to the ground. Five construction workers died.

Taiwan sits right on an active earthquake fault. That means earthquakes occur fairly often. During a 6.6 magnitude earthquake in December 2003, the building swayed. Fortunately, no damage was reported.

How did engineers make Taipei 101 safe? They did it by putting a giant, 680-ton steel ball on the building's eighty-eighth floor. When the building sways one way, the ball's extra weight pulls it back in the opposite direction. The architects left the gold-painted ball exposed for people to see.

The building's design is based on the Chinese lucky number 8. The middle of the jade-green, 101-story building rises in eight slanted sections. Its shape is inspired by bamboo. Bamboo symbolizes sturdiness. The building also has the world's fastest elevators. They zoom at 38 miles per hour. Visitors reach the ninetieth floor in just 39 seconds.

Taipei 101 will probably not be the world champion for height for very long. South Korea, China, Hong Kong, and India have taller towers already in the works. There's another tower being built in the United States, too. This tower will replace and memorialize the World Trade Center. It will be taller than them all.

Chapter 6

9/11 and Beyond

On September 11, 2001, nearly 3,000 people were killed when the twin towers of the World Trade Center collapsed in a cloud of smoke and ash. The terrorist attacks on the skyscrapers were the worst ever carried out in the United States. No one can forget the images of that tragic day. No one can forget the heart-wrenching weeks that followed. The two huge skyscrapers were gone. In their place was a huge hole. In the aftermath, many Americans were determined to rebuild.

The people of New York City came up with a plan. They put together a group of people. This group was called the Lower Manhattan Development Corporation (LMDC). The LMDC began a worldwide search for architects in the summer of 2002. The architects would give their ideas for a new skyscraper to be built on the World Trade Center site. These architects had a serious challenge. They needed to **internalize** what had happened. Then they had to somehow express it in their building plans. They needed to transform the site from a place of tragedy into a place where the loss is remembered. They needed to turn it into a place where life, freedom, and hope are celebrated.

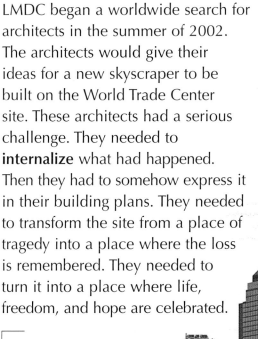

The World Trade Center

Emotions Run High

The competition had some **restrictions**. Each architect had to propose a bold new skyline. Each had to include a memorial for the victims. The buildings would also have to be used in several ways, such as offices, stores, and housing.

As the contest **progressed**, the LMDC received 406 entries from architects around the globe. From those, the LMDC narrowed the search to seven teams. These teams included the world's most-talented architects, planners, and designers. The competition was intense. By December 2002, the judges had selected nine designs. How would they choose a winner?

Before making a decision, the corporation reached out to the public. They displayed the nine designs. The display drew 100,000 visitors! Millions of other people looked at the plans on the Internet. Newspapers ran pictures of all the designs. Public meetings were held in New York and neighboring New Jersey. The plans were evaluated based on several factors: How well does the site provide an appropriate memorial? Is the building attractive? How much will it cost? What does the public think? Some people thought the designs were cold and impersonal. Others broke down and cried at the sight of the designs. Many families of victims opposed any building on the site at all. To them, the ground was sacred.

The LMDC reviewed thousands of comments from the public. In February 2003, it selected two finalists. One finalist was "Memory **Foundations**," by the architect Daniel Libeskind. The other finalist was the "World Cultural Center" by a group called THINK Design. Both plans proposed bold, new skyscrapers. Both designs placed a memorial—rather than office towers—in the center of their design.

The THINK team proposed new, soaring twin towers that would border the **foundations** of the original buildings. The new towers would be made of an open web of cables, inspired by the Eiffel Tower. Within these towers, buildings would be constructed. They could house a museum, performing arts center, and other public spaces.

The judges liked this design a lot. However, Libeskind's proposal won the competition. The centerpiece of his winning design is the Freedom Tower. It is a 70-story office tower with a **progressive** twist upward. Above the office space is a 350-foot weblike structure. It resembles the cables of the Brooklyn Bridge. This area will house a group of wind turbines to produce power. The entire structure is topped by a 276-foot spire. It points to the sky just like the raised arm of the Statue of Liberty. The structure climbs a total of 1,776 feet, a symbol of the year that the United States claimed its independence. When it is built, the Freedom Tower will be the tallest skyscraper in the world.

An illustration of the proposed memorial for those lost at the World Trade Center. Two large spaces that contain pools of water outline the footprints of the twin towers.

High Anxiety

Some people will debate the "world's tallest" claim. Why? Only the first 70 floors of the Freedom Tower will be **occupied** by people. The bigger question on everyone's mind, though, is safety. After all, anyone who enters the new building will surely think back to the events of September 11, 2001. Many might even worry that tragedy could strike again.

Libeskind's design partner, David Childs, has responded to this worry. He said that the Freedom Tower would "probably be the safest building in the world." The designers want to make sure that building safety is more than **adequate**. They are trying to imagine worst-case scenarios. They plan to use the best technology available to make sure that the building will survive and that the people inside will be safe.

Libeskind and Childs's plan includes strengthening the steel structure of Memory **Foundations**. They will add concrete stairwells that can withstand a blast. They also plan to install biological and chemical air filters and to simulate evacuations. Their goal is to exceed New York City's building safety laws. The building designers want this tower to be a model of safety for future skyscrapers.

The Freedom Tower will be "green." That doesn't mean it will be painted green. It means that the building will be environmentally friendly. New skyscrapers across the United States are already using solar power, recycled building materials, and other "green" features. The Freedom Tower's wind turbines will provide about 20 percent of the building's energy. The heating and air-conditioning systems will be designed to save energy. The building will also **utilize** recycled rainwater.

The ground breaking of the Freedom Tower's **foundation** took place on July 4, 2004. A ground breaking is the "official" start of a big building project. The goal is to complete the building by September 11, 2009. On that date, another related project will also be completed: the memorial for those who died in the World Trade Center attack.

More than 5,200 people from 63 countries entered a contest to build the memorial. All of the designs were displayed online for the public to see. People from around the world expressed their emotions in creative and sometimes offbeat ways. One suggested a sculpture of a giant red question mark asking *When? Who? What?* and *Why?* Another displayed a sculpture of a massive, weeping giant.

In January 2004, judges announced the winner. Designed by architects Michael Arad and Peter Walker, the memorial is called "Reflecting Absence." It is surrounded by a field of trees, and it has two large square-shaped voids. These empty spaces will be where the World Trade Center once stood. The empty spaces will contain pools of water. The designers say the voids are visible reminders of the tremendous loss brought by the attacks on the World Trade Center.

A pair of ramps will border each pool. The ramps will lead down to a memorial space. Visitors will walk down the ramps in cool darkness. At the bottom, they will see another pool of water. It will be surrounded by a continuous ribbon that lists the names of the victims. Visitors will be able to view many preserved artifacts, such as a crushed fire truck. There will also be lecture halls and a library. As the designers propose, "Reflecting Absence" will be a **meaningful**, living part of the new skyscraper, and the city itself.

A Look to the Future

Some people say that modern technology could allow buildings to climb higher than 3,000 feet. That height is twice as tall as the Petronas Towers. Yet the World Trade Center attacks have some people asking: Do we really need taller buildings?

As of yet, no one has plans to build a superscraper that is 3,000 feet tall. First, safety would always be a concern. Second, the taller the building, the higher the cost would be. Third, these superscrapers would sway so much in the wind that the people inside might feel sick. Fourth, it would take elevators an awfully long time to reach the highest floors in the building. Finally, such a building would block light and views for miles around its neighborhood.

At the same time, architects continue to build taller and taller buildings. It's hard to hold back the human desire to reach for the sky. As you've read, skyscrapers can rise as symbols of hope, **progress**, and renewal. As long as skyscrapers remain powerful symbols, humankind will continue to reach for the stars.

An artist's rendering of the proposed monument at the World Trade Center site

GLOSSARY

adequate sufficient or enough for a specific requirement.
Inadequate means not enough.

architects people whose job involves designing buildings.
Architectural means related to the design of buildings.

confining able to keep an object within tight or narrow limits.
The **confine**s of a place are its borders.

consisting being composed or made up of

consumed to have eaten or used up an item. **Consumed** also
means to give full attention to or be absorbed with something.

destructive hurtful or damaging. **Destruction** is the act of
destroying an object.

essential basic, indispensable, necessary; fundamental or vital
to a thing's existence. **Essentially** means basically.

foundation the underlying base or support of a structure; the
basis or principle upon which something stands

ideal a part of a person's belief system. An **ideal** can also be
the best example of something.

immovable not able to be moved or relocated. **Movable**
means able to be moved or relocated.

internalize to make something a part of one's own patterns of
thinking. **Internal** means inside.

involved to have taken part or had a role in an act

leadership the rulers of a group of people. **Leadership** also
means guidance or direction.

lessen to shrink in degree or number; decrease

luxuries items that provide great comfort but that are usually not affordable for most people. **Luxurious** means rich or lavish.

meaningful having a purpose

modify to make a change in something

occupants those who occupy space, such as tenants. **Occupancy** means the taking up or filling of a space.

partially partly, or not completely

passages paths through an enclosed area. A **passage** can also mean a journey. A **passageway** is another word for path.

portable capable of being moved or carried

possess to have an object or to own it. A **possession** is an object that belongs to a person.

profession a career that requires special training. A **professional** is a person who has special training for a career.

progressive making use of new ideas. **Progressed** means moved forward. **Progress** can also mean a forward movement.

prominent readily noticeable; widely known

realm a particular area, often an area ruled over by a king

reluctant not eager to act

resembled looked like something or someone else. A **resemblance** is a likeness to something else.

resolve to determine. A person's **resolve** means his or her determination to do something.

restrict to limit. A **restriction** is a limitation.

tomb a burial place for a dead person

utilize to make use of

INDEX